Scatalog

A Kid's Field Guide to Animal Poop

How to Track a Hippo

Henry Owens

"Because Everybody Poops"

Windmill Books
New York

Published in 2014 by Windmill Books, An Imprint of Rosen Publishing
29 East 21st Street, New York, NY 10010

First Edition

Editor: Amelie von Zumbusch
Photo Research: Katie Stryker
Book Design: Colleen Bialecki

Photo Credits: Cover (top) robbosphotos/Shutterstock.com; cover (bottom), p. 16 W. Van Amerongen/Flickr; background Schankz/Shutterstock.com; p. 5 Leon Marais/Shutterstock.com; p. 6 PlusONE/Shutterstock.com; p. 8 Visuals Unlimited, Inc/Robert Pickett/Getty Images; p. 9 Neale Cousland/Shutterstock.com; p. 11 Graeme Shannon/Shutterstock.com; p. 12 Manoj Shah/The Image Bank/Getty Images; p. 13 yiq/Shutterstock.com; pp. 15, 17 (right) Mogens Trolle/Shutterstock.com; p. 17 (right) Bobby Childs/Flickr; p. 18 Mint Images-Frans Lanting/The Agency Collection/Getty Images; p. 19 Jiri Haureljuk/Shutterstock.com; p. 21 Christian Heeb/AWL Images/Getty Images; p. 22 Colby Lyons/Flickr.

Library of Congress Cataloging-in-Publication Data

Owens, Henry.
How to track a hippo / by Henry Owens. — First edition.
pages cm. — (Scatalog: a kid's field guide to animal poop)
Includes index.
ISBN 978-1-61533-888-7 (library) — ISBN 978-1-61533-894-8 (pbk.) —
ISBN 978-1-61533-900-6 (6-pack)
1. Hippopotamus—Juvenile literature. 2. Animal droppings—Juvenile literature. I. Title.
QL737.U57O94 2014
599.63'5—dc23

2013029218

Manufactured in the United States of America

CPSIA Compliance Information: Batch # BW14WM: For Further Information contact Windmill Books Publishing, New York, New York at 1-866-478-0556

CONTENTS

ON THE LOOKOUT FOR HIPPOS

The word "hippopotamus" comes from the Greek words for "river horse." Hippos do not look much like horses, though. These creatures are one of the largest land animals on Earth. They are one of the deadliest, too. In fact, hippos kill more than 2,500 people every year.

If you were walking through hippo **habitat**, how would you track, or find and follow, a hippo? Scientists and safari guides use many methods to track animals in the wild. It may sound gross, but one of the best ways to track a hippo is by looking for its poop!

An adult hippo can weigh between 5,000 and 8,000 pounds (2,268–3,629 kg). As most big animals do, hippos produce a lot of poop. Hippo poop is also called dung.

WHERE TO FIND HIPPOS

If you plan to track a hippo, you will need to visit sub-Saharan Africa. This is the part of Africa that is south of a big desert called the Sahara. Hippos make their homes in sub-Saharan Africa's rivers and lakes. Many of Africa's hippos live in **wildlife refuges** and other places where they are protected.

These hippos live in Botswana's Chobe National Park. The park has a healthy hippo population. It is a great place to visit if you want to track hippos.

Hippos can spend up to 16 hours a day in the water! This helps them stay cool in Africa's hot **climate**. When it is time to eat, hippos leave the water. They graze on the grasses of the **savanna**. Savannas are grassy plains with few trees or bushes.

A BODY BUILT FOR WATER

To spot a hippo in a river or lake, look carefully at the water's surface. Hippos often keep just their eyes, ears, and nostrils out of the water. Their eyes, ears, and nostrils are all near the tops of their heads. This lets hippos breathe and keep watch when they are mostly underwater.

Hippos move easily through the water. However, they don't swim much. Instead, they walk or bound along the bottom of a lake or river.

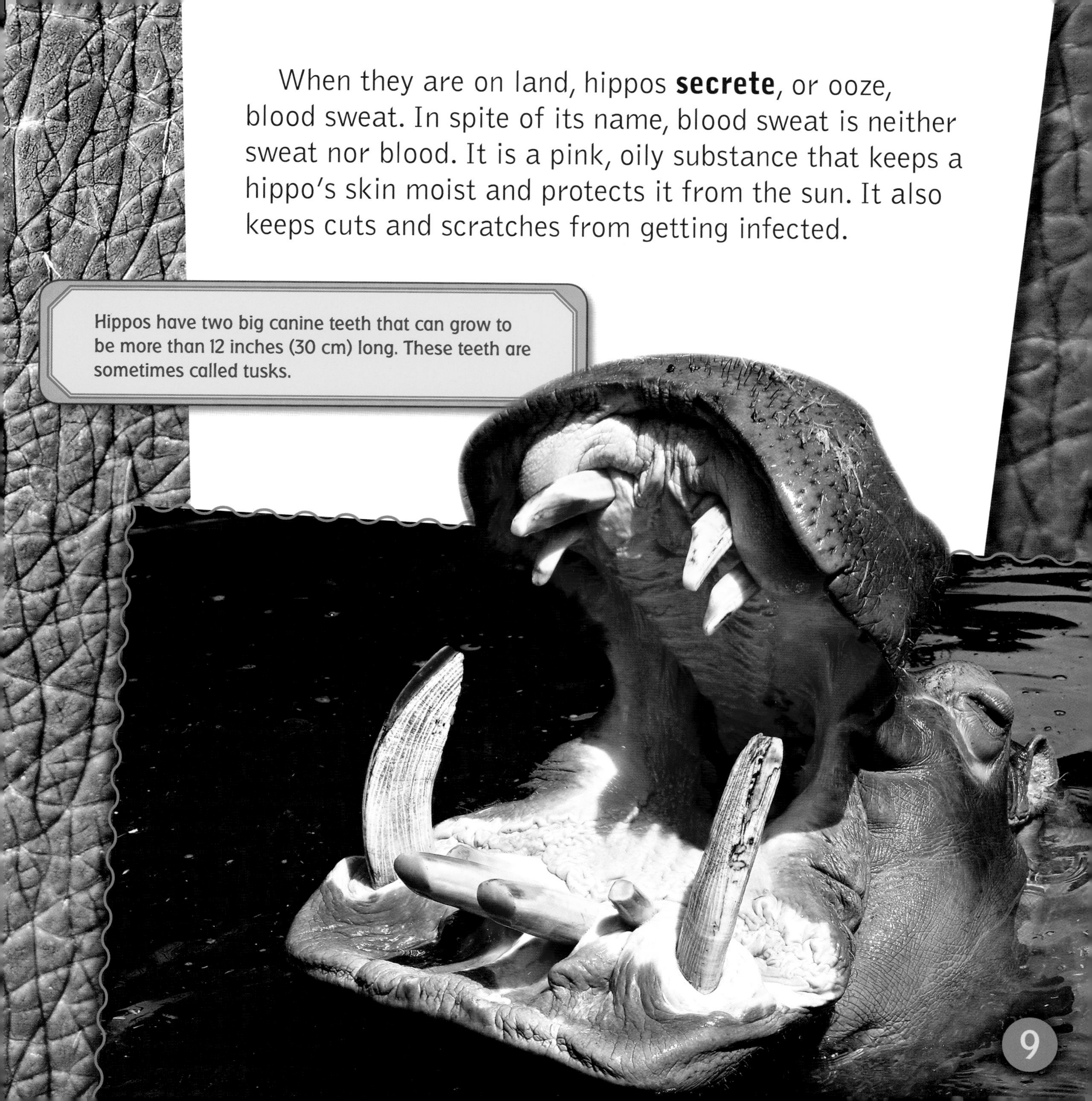

When they are on land, hippos **secrete**, or ooze, blood sweat. In spite of its name, blood sweat is neither sweat nor blood. It is a pink, oily substance that keeps a hippo's skin moist and protects it from the sun. It also keeps cuts and scratches from getting infected.

Hippos have two big canine teeth that can grow to be more than 12 inches (30 cm) long. These teeth are sometimes called tusks.

LISTENING FOR HIPPOS

Always keep your ears open when tracking hippos. Listen for the grunts, bellows, and mooing sounds that hippos make to **communicate** with each other. Hippos can hear sounds through both air and water.

Hippos live in herds of about 10 to 15 members. A herd is made up of a **dominant** male, several females, and their young. Males are **territorial** when they are in water. When another male gets too close to a herd, the herd's male will open his mouth and show his large teeth. If the other male does not leave, the two hippos will fight.

Hippo fights can be very loud. Hippos grunt and roar when they are fighting. They also open their mouths wide to show off their big teeth.

FINDING BABY HIPPOS

If you're really lucky, you might spot a baby hippo, or calf. Calves can weigh as much as 100 pounds (45 kg) when they are born. Some calves are born on land, while others are born in the water. When a calf is born underwater, its mother pushes it to the surface to breathe.

People tracking hippos must be extra careful when calves are nearby. Mother hippos will attack anything or anyone that they think is a threat to their calves.

Hippo calves often eat their own dung. Hippo dung is full of nutrients, or things that living things need to live and grow. Adult hippos sometimes eat hippo dung, too.

Even though they spend their days in water, hippos are **mammals**. As all mammals do, baby hippos drink their mothers' milk. Hippo calves can nurse underwater. This is because they have special flaps that seal their eyes and nostrils closed. These flaps even allow hippos to sleep underwater.

BIG POOP PRODUCERS

Hippos are **herbivores**. This means they eat only plants. Hippos feed mostly on grasses. They sometimes eat fruit, too. Hippos rely on their four-part stomachs, large intestines, and small intestines to **digest** food. The parts of a hippo's stomach are the right diverticulum, left diverticulum, anterior stomach, and posterior stomach.

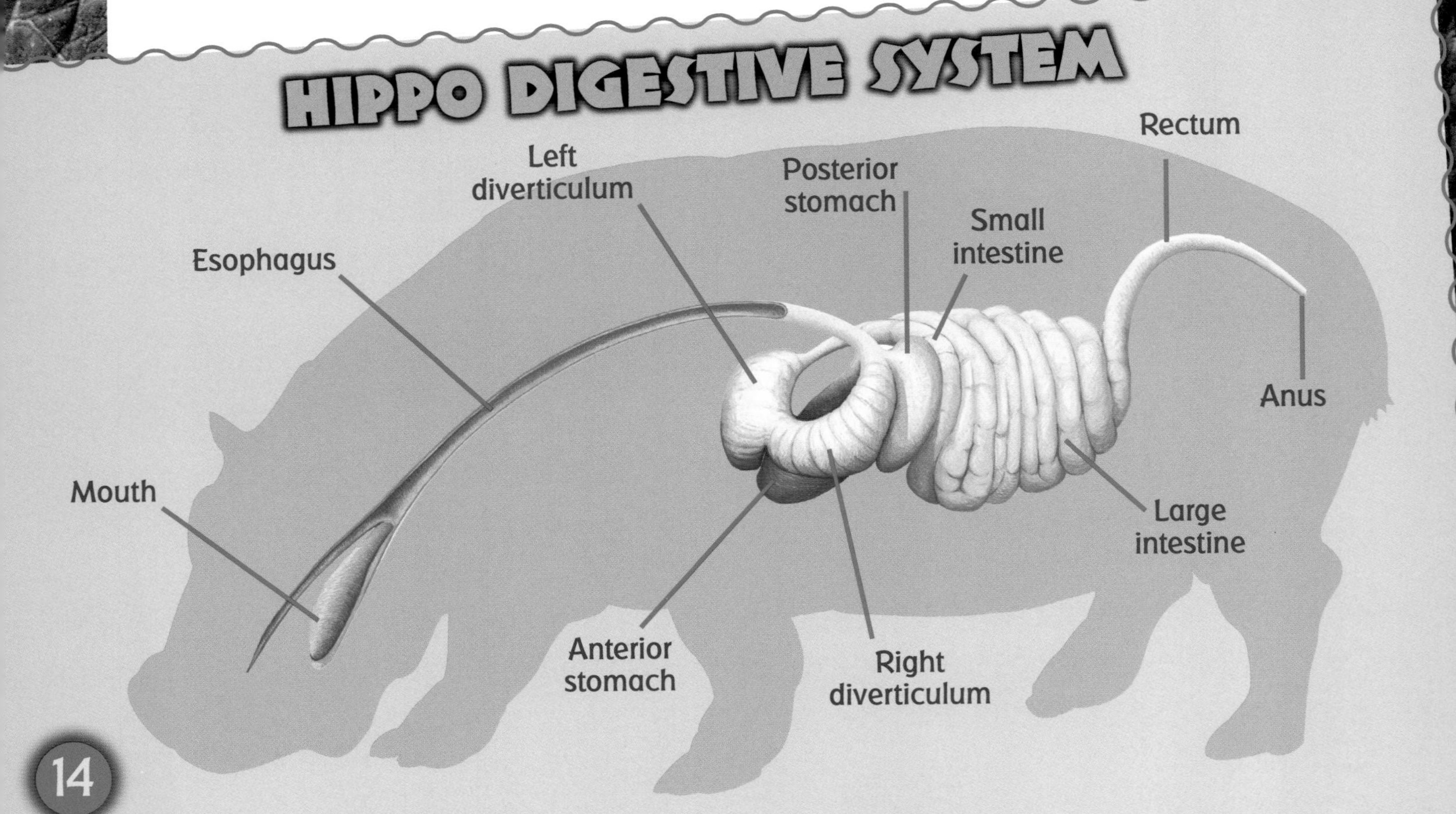

Hippos often return to favorite grazing spots, called hippo lawns. The grass there becomes short from so much grazing. If you find a hippo lawn, hippos are likely nearby.

Every evening, hippos leave their rivers and lakes. They move to land and graze on the grasses of the savanna. Hippos may travel as far as 6 miles (10 km) looking for food. In one night, a hippo can eat as much as 80 pounds (36 kg) of grass. All that food means that hippos make a lot of poop! An adult hippo can produce 60 pounds (27 kg) of poop every day.

POOP WITH A PURPOSE

If you want to find hippos, look for hippo dung. Male hippos use dung to mark their territories. They leave big piles of dung, called middens. They also show off their dominance by whipping their tails quickly back and forth as they poop, flinging dung in every direction. This display is called dung showering.

Lumps of hippo dung usually measure about 8 inches (20 cm) across. You can sometimes see bits of grass in them.

DUNG AND HIPPO TERRITORIES

MIDDENS

- Found on paths leading into and out of a male's territory.
- Males add poop to the pile several times each day.

DUNG SHOWERING

- Happens at the borders of territories.
- Males stand facing different directions and start flinging poop everywhere.

Since hippos spend most of their time in water, a lot of their dung ends up there. In the water, hippo poop is a food for tiny creatures called microorganisms. Worms and **larvae** eat these microorganisms. Fish eat the worms and larvae. Many animals depend on hippo dung!

TRACKING TIPS

On land, hippos often travel along narrow, worn paths. Looking for the deep ruts of their paths is one way to track them. Keep an eye out for piles of dung near the paths, too. Looking at the dung can give you an idea of how many hippos are in an area and when they passed through.

Some safaris, or animal-watching trips, teach guests tracking skills. These people used their tracking skills to find a herd of hippos in Zambia's Luangwa Valley.

Scientists use many methods to track animals. Some of these methods, such as radio collars, do not work well with hippos. Hippos are difficult to catch and are very dangerous to humans. Studying hippos' poop is a much safer way to learn about them.

HIPPOS IN DANGER

In some parts of Africa, hippos are hard to track because their numbers are dropping fast. This is especially true in Virunga National Park, in the Democratic Republic of the Congo. Between 2006 and 2010, about 95 percent of the park's hippos were killed. This was mostly due to **poaching**, or illegal killing. Poachers generally kill hippos for their meat and canine teeth.

Habitat loss is also a threat to hippos. As people move closer into hippos' habitats, there are fewer resources for the animals. People also build dams, which change the flow of rivers and destroy hippos' homes.

Today, most hippos live in protected areas, such as national parks and wildlife refuges. These people are watching hippos in Botswana's Chobe National Park.

"FISH EAGLE II"

STAYING SAFE

If you ever find yourself near one of Africa's rivers or lakes, look out for hippos. If you see hippo poop or other signs of these huge animals, keep your distance and be careful. Hippos are aggressive and will often attack humans.

However, hippos are also important to the **ecosystems** in which they live. Hippo dung helps keep animals living in rivers and lakes alive. If hippos were to die out, these animals would be in danger, too!

Another reason not to get too close to a hippo is to avoid getting hit by a dung shower.

GLOSSARY

climate (KLY-mut) The kind of weather a certain place has.

communicate (kuh-MYOO-nih-kayt) To share facts or feelings.

digest (dy-JEST) To break down food so that the body can use it.

dominant (DAH-mih-nent) In charge.

ecosystems (EE-koh-sis-temz) Communities of living things and the surroundings in which they live.

habitat (HA-buh-tat) The kind of land where an animal or a plant naturally lives.

herbivores (ER-buh-vorz) Animals that eat only plants.

larvae (LAHR-vee) Animals in the early period of life in which they have a wormlike form.

mammals (MA-mulz) Warm-blooded animals that have backbones and hair, breathe air, and feed milk to their young.

poaching (POHCH-ing) Hunting animals when it is against the law.

savanna (suh-VA-nuh) A grassland with few trees or bushes.

secrete (sih-KREET) To make a liquid or a gas and then let it out.

territorial (ter-uh-TAWR-ee-ul) Guarding land or space for its own use.

wildlife refuges (WYLD-lyf REH-fyooj-ez) Places that give protection to animals.

INDEX

WEBSITES

For web resources related to the subject of this book, go to:
www.windmillbooks.com/weblinks and select this book's title.